RUSTIC RECIPES
THE WOODBURNER COOKBOOK

JENNIFER LUNENBORG

COUNTRY BOOKS

Published by Country Books/Ashridge Press
Courtyard Cottage, Little Longstone, Bakewell, Derbyshire DE45 1NN
Tel: 01629 640670
e-mail: dickrichardson@country-books.co.uk
www.countrybooks.biz

ISBN 978-1-910489-60-4

British Library Cataloguing in Publication Data.
A catalogue record for this book is available from the British Library

Printed and bound in England by 4edge Ltd.

CONTENTS

ACKNOWLEDGEMENTS   4

CHAPTER 1 – INTRODUCTION   5

CHAPTER 2 – THE EVOLUTION OF THE WOODBURNER 9

CHAPTER 3 – SOUP   11

CHAPTER 4 – SAVOURY DISHES   17

CHAPTER 5 – ACCOMPANIMENTS   30

CHAPTER 6 – PUDDINGS   38

CHAPTER 7 – FESTIVE RECIPES: PART I   43

CHAPTER 7 – FESTIVE RECIPES: PART II   48

CHAPTER 8 – BASICS   53

CHAPTER 9 – FORAGING   58

RECIPE INDEX   69

BIBLIOGRAPHY   70

ACKNOWLEDGEMENTS

First and foremost I would like to thank my husband Bert Lunenborg for all his support and encouragement, without his constant reassurance I would not have completed this book. My thanks also go to my mum, Leila Lauder, for her proofreading skills. Despite being a freelance proofreader myself, a second pair of eyes is incredibly useful, particularly when proofreading one's own work. For the photography I would like to thank Eugen Frantiu, as well as my father John Lauder, and once again my husband. Yurt photo was taken on holiday in the Netherlands, at Jurre's beautiful yurt in Anna Paulowna, Noord Holland. Finally my four children, Emily, Ollie, Lottie and Amelia for not only trying most of the dishes in this book, but also for their patience waiting for supper after a long day at school or college. Along with my children, my thanks also goes to our French student, Ouns El Harzli, who I hope also enjoyed many of these dishes during his six month stay with us.

CHAPTER 1
INTRODUCTION

Life is getting more and more driven by technology, we use our phones to wake us up in the morning, and continue to use them throughout the day, relying on them for email, internet, gps, calculator, and numerous other activities. Our lives are fast, stressful and dependent on technology to simply assist us in many basic tasks.

Think back to a simpler time, when life was about family, preparing food, cooking, sitting together in the evenings all in one room, usually because they could only afford to heat one room, but communicating, young and old together. Then think of today, some families don't even own a dining table, many families eat at separate times, in front of the tv, in bedrooms on devices, is this progress! We don't know our own children, or what they are watching, particularly as they become teenagers.

We don't want to step back in time, life is not all bad today, people live longer, there are more cures for disease, more disposable income; but we can learn from the past, take the best of both worlds.

Every now and then we experience power cuts, without electricity and gas, how do we eat hot food. It is ok if a power failure occurs in the Summer months, we simply barbecue and eat salads for a day or two, knowing the power will return shortly. But what about in the Winter, when it is cold, rainy, miserable outside, we need hot food to keep us warm, particularly if the power failure has resulted in a lack of heating our home.

We had such a power failure for three weeks, in October last year. Both my husband and I were too busy with work to find the fault, or even take time off work to get an electrician in, so we improvised. This is the story of how a family of six, plus our French student, and an additional three children staying every weekend not only survived, but thrived with very limited cooking facilities.

For one we are lucky enough to have a flat top woodburner, bought deliberately so tea/coffee/hot chocolate could be made in the event of a power failure. But this became our major cooking source for those three weeks.

The following book gives examples of what can be achieved when necessary. We didn't eat a bland diet of sandwiches and salad, we experimented with a variety of recipes, some more successful than others, and learnt patience. The wood had to be collected, our six year old, took this on as her role, the fire started, the woodburner needed to warm up before cooking and there was no way of controlling the heat once warmed, so food had to be monitored more closely. After a long day at work, three adults, two teenagers and two hungry children, learnt to sit together, took turns watching the food cook, chat and become more of a family than we had been in a while.

To begin with we ate simply, jacket potatoes cooked in the woodburner, the first time they were wrapped in a single layer of silver foil, this evidently wasn't sufficient as they were scorched by the heat of the flames, the centre still being edible but the skin not so. So we learnt to wrap them in triple layers of foil and place them in a small cake tray on top of the woodburner, so they didn't touch direct heat. After that they were delicious.

Despite very limited cooking facilities we did have a fridge and freezer during this time as we weren't completely without power, so some short cuts were taken, ie I bought ready-made pastry, for example, but all recipes could be adapted in the event of no power, additional basic recipes, such as pastry, can be found in Chapter 8.

Let me start by saying that I am the last person who should be writing a recipe book; it's not that I don't love to cook, I do, but I rarely stick to a recipe. I use recipes as a guide to give me ideas, then adapt them to suit our family's' tastes, or more often, to suit what we have in the kitchen cupboards. I regularly swap honey for syrup, and vice versa, they are of a very similar consistency, and my honey flap-jacks, are now much preferred by the family, to the more usual syrup based flapjacks. If a recipe mentions herbs or spices, I see what we have on the dresser. I don't swap herbs for spices, but in my humble opinion, cinnamon, ginger, mixed spice and allspice are all quite interchangeable

Before I start detailing recipes using a woodburner, let's start with the basics. For most of us, a cup of tea or coffee first thing in the morning is not only part of our morning ritual, for some of us it is an almost essential ingredient to a successful day. Both my husband and I are coffee drinkers, preferring freshly brewed coffee, or a cappuccino to the instant variety. On a woodburner achieving a cappuccino is beyond my capabilities, but using an Italian style stovetop coffee pot makes very good coffee, alternatively, boiling a kettle on the woodburner and making coffee using a cafetiere is also quite acceptable. My three older children on the other hand, tend to prefer tea to coffee, again using a stovetop kettle and a cast iron tea pot to keep the tea warm once made is not only possible, but fun too. Our youngest prefers hot chocolate, again very easy on a woodburner, and extra yummy if you only add mini marshmallows as a treat when made this way. So hot drinks all round, but what kettle should you use on your woodburner?

Traditionally copper kettles have been used since 1893, the copper conducts heat much better than stainless steel, however, copper kettles should only be used on a medium heat, not a problem on a woodburner as the kettle sits on top, not inside the fire box, but because of this, they use less energy than other types of kettle, and if you are already using the woodburner to heat your home, no extra energy at all. If you don't have a copper kettle, any stovetop kettle will do the job; alternatively a saucepan with water in is an easy option open to all.

Let me finish this section by adding that although all of the recipes in this book have been tried and tested on our woodburner, they can all equally be made using more conventional cooking methods. When you have time, cooking on the woodburner is fun, when you are without power, cooking on the woodburner is vital. I would suggest that every now and then you attempt some of the following recipes on your woodburner, so you know how to cook this way if and when the need arises. You may like to experiment with some of these recipes conventionally, so you know in advance which recipes you prefer. Either way, whether you use this book as a bible, following the recipes and cooking methods to a tee, or you use this book as a rough guide, helping when necessary and giving ideas when not. I hope you will find it useful.

CHAPTER 2
THE EVOLUTION OF THE WOODBURNER

It was not until the end of the 18th Century that the design of the woodburner was improved to resemble the modern day wood-burner, in fact, America's founding father Benjamin Franklin, had a go at developing his own unique cast iron stove in 1744.

Woodburning stoves, as opposed to open fires, have a number of benefits, they are relatively dirt-free, they have an in-built draught which means you get a fierce blaze, and as a result they are 80 per cent more efficient than an open fire.

We live in the countryside, without mains gas, where wood-burners are a popular source of heating homes, combined with the huge increase in families purchasing their own small woodlands, more and more people have a ready supply of free wood.

Woodburners have developed over the years becoming more and more efficient, to a point where today's woodburners draw air across the door of the stove, creating a barrier between the burning fuel and the glass, this not only keeps the temperature in the woodburner high, it also keeps the glass door clean. This efficiency also means that less wood is required to heat the woodburner, resulting in less cost, less air pollution, and less hassle, (you don't need to buy or collect as much wood), and as long as sustainable wood is used, the worries about deforestation are eliminated and thus the woodburner appeals to many as an environmentally friendly alternative to traditional energy supplies.

In fact in 2009 when gas companies drastically increased their prices, and fears about Russia turning off the pipeline to Britain altogether became a real worry, woodburners were marketed as an environmentally friendly, cheaper alternative to heating one's home.

It has therefore been only the past 9 years that the woodburner has become an iconic status symbol of the middles classes, in fact Harry Wallop in his book *Consumed* quotes David Spencer at the Stove Industry Alliance, "200,000 wood-burners were installed in 2014, with close to one million homes in Britain now having one".

Harry Wallop also quotes Michael Czerwinski at the Design Museum as saying: "It is all part of a complex, romantic harking back to the Seventies Good Life movement. In a sophisticated, dangerous world we are looking to a more simple way of living". This quote pretty much sums up everything this book is about, trying to reconnect with ourselves, our families and nature.

CHAPTER 3
SOUP

Soup is one of the easiest dishes to cook on a woodburner, I have included a couple of recipes, but generally when it comes to making soup, you can chuck in any vegetable lurking in the fridge, some go better with others, ie red onions go particularly well with tomatoes, mushrooms are best used to make a mushroom soup only rather than being thrown into a mixed vegetable soup as they tend to make the soup a little grey, which isn't aesthetically very pleasing, lentils and potatoes can be used as a filler, if you want a hearty soup. I have even been known to make stinging nettle soup, not my favourite, but very edible if you like foraging.

Celery Soup
Carrot Soup
Minestrone Soup
French Onion Soup
Chicken Soup
Pumpkin Soup (see Chapter 7 Festive Recipes, Part ii Halloween)
Stinging Nettle Soup (see Chapter 9 Foraging)

CELERY SOUP

Unfortunately it is an urban myth that you use more calories to eat and digest celery than it contains. However, administered for anti-hypertension in folk medicine for centuries, celery still has many cardiovascular benefits. It demonstrates both antioxidant and anti-inflammatory properties that help improve blood pressure and cholesterol levels, as well as preventing heart disease. It also provides dietary fibre that boosts digestion and weight loss. Containing high quantities of water and electrolytes, celery can prevent dehydration and compounds present in it work as a diuretic. In addition providing antioxidant flavonoids and polyphenol phytonutrients, eating celery can also improve liver, skin, eye and cognitive health. And with only 25 calories in two sticks of celery, this wonder food shouldn't be overlooked.

Ingredients
1 white onion, chopped
4-5 sticks of celery, sliced
1 pint / 570ml of vegetable stock, using either a stock cube or stock pot
1 tbsp extra virgin olive oil
1 dash of cream (optional)

celery.

Method
Chop the vegetables and place in a large pan with the olive oil on the woodburner, when the vegetables are soft, add the stock, and simmer till ready. Add a dash of cream and serve with home-made bread rolls, see Chapter 5.

CARROT SOUP

Carrots were domesticated over 5000 years ago and today there are over 100 species. In fact until the 17th Century, the only edible carrots were black, white, red or purple, the iconic orange carrots that we enjoy today, were created in the Netherlands, as a tribute to the ruling House of Orange, as my Dutch husband likes to remind me. Amongst all of the vegetables, carrots contain the largest amount of beta carotene, ie Vitamin A, which promotes good vision and eye health, hence the commonly held belief that you will be able to see in the dark if you eat your carrots, not completely true but not far off.

Ingredients
1 white onion, chopped
3 carrots, chopped
1 pint/570ml of vegetable stock, using either a stock cube or stock pot
1 tbsp extra virgin olive oil

Method
Chop the vegetables and place in a large pan with the olive oil on the woodburner, when the vegetables are soft, add the stock, and simmer till ready. Serve with home-made bread rolls, see Chapter 5.

MINESTRONE SOUP

Minestrone is an Italian soup made with fresh seasonal vegetables, often but not exclusively with pasta or rice added. The most common ingredients are beans, onions, carrots, celery and stock, as well as pasta or rice, but as there is no set recipe for minestrone soup, you can add whatever vegetables you have in store, or even add meat to the recipe. Originally minestrone soup was made with leftovers, and was generally a meal in itself for the poorer members of Italian society as it was filling, cheap and wholesome. But today in both Italy and all over the world, it is made as a dish in its own right, usually as a starter.

Ingredients

1 white onion, chopped
1 carrot, chopped
1 stick of celery, sliced
¼ white cabbage, sliced
1 pinch of Italian herbs or mixed dried herbs
Handful of spaghetti
Handful of peas/sweetcorn
1 pint/570ml of vegetable stock, using either a stock cube or stock pot
1 tbsp extra virgin olive oil

Method

Chop the vegetables and place in a large pan with the olive oil on the woodburner, when the vegetables are soft stir in the herbs, add the stock and spaghetti, and simmer till ready. Serve with home-made bread rolls or garlic bread; see Chapter 5, for a truly Italian meal.

FRENCH ONION SOUP

The French are still caricatured in the UK as wearing berets, stripy tops and cycling around with onions around their necks, but where does this originate? The French are often surprised by this image, as only a minority of Frenchmen actually wore berets. The image in fact took roots in the UK back in the 1800s when a number of Frenchmen from Brittany who were dressed in their regional dress of stripy tops and berets came to the UK to sell onions, and since they were the only Frenchmen many English came into contact with, they assumed that all Frenchmen dressed this way. However, strings of onions were heavy, and so once bicycles were introduced in the 1930s, it made it easier to string the onions over a pole carried on their shoulders and cycle around than it did to walk. As a popular name in Brittany at the time was Yann, which in English is John, the French onion sellers were referred to as 'Onion Johnnies' and by 1929, there were 1,400 'Onion Johnnies' selling 9,000 tonnes of onions in the UK.

Ingredients
3 white onions, finely chopped
1 pinch of herbs from Provence or mixed dried herbs
1 pint/570ml of vegetable stock, using either a stock cube or stock pot
1 tbsp extra virgin olive oil

Method
Place the onions in a large pan with the olive oil on the woodburner, when the onions are soft add the herbs, I prefer to use herbs from Provence, to give a truly French aroma to the soup, but any mixed dried herbs will do, add the stock, and simmer till ready. Serve with home-made bread rolls, see Chapter 5.

CHICKEN SOUP

Chicken soup has long been considered a folk remedy for colds and flu and back in the 12th Century, a Jewish physician Maimonides, even recommended chicken soup for curing leprosy and asthma. It is still referred to today as the 'Jewish penicillin'. I don't claim that the following recipe will be a cure-all, but my family certainly enjoy a bowl of home-made chicken soup on a cold Winter's day.

I wouldn't recommend cooking a whole chicken from scratch on a woodburner, however, sometimes a power cut occurs and you have cooked chicken in the fridge which will need using up. Alternatively as we were without power for 3 weeks, I resorted to buying whole cooked chicken and using that for a variety of recipes, my only regret was I usually buy free-range chicken, and I couldn't find free-range whole cooked chicken in the supermarkets, but in less than ideal circumstances, needs must, and feeding the family a variety of wholesome, home-cooked meals, overtook my morals for only buying free-range for a couple of weeks. I was still able to buy free-range eggs, as you can boil eggs on a woodburner, however, I would like to think you don't need a recipe for boiling an egg! But please note, when boiling an egg on the woodburner, you do need to ensure the woodburner is roaring, as just ticking over won't boil an egg, I know this from experience.

Ingredients
1 white onion, chopped, if you have a leftover roast chicken, use the onion which was used to stuff the chicken
1 carrot, chopped
Handful of peas/sweetcorn
3oz/75g egg noodles
1 pint/570ml of chicken stock, using either a stock cube or stock pot
1 tbsp extra virgin olive oil

Method
Place the vegetables in a large pan with the olive oil on the woodburner, when the vegetables are soft, add the whole chicken carcass, noodles and stock, and simmer. Prior to serving, take the carcass out of the pan, and remove all chicken meat from the bird and add back to the soup. Serve with home-made bread rolls, see Chapter 5.

CHAPTER 4
SAVOURY DISHES

According to the *Oxford English Dictionary* Online, the definition of 'savoury' when referring to food, is "belonging to the category that is salty or spicy rather than sweet". I'm not sure I completely agree with this definition, in that not all savoury food is either salty or spicy, and in fact some savoury food, curries made with coconut milk and apricots, or ham and pineapple pizza, to name but a few, can be quite sweet. Originating from the Middle English word 'savouri', which is ultimately based on the old French word 'savoure', which simply means 'tasty'. I like to think all of the dishes in this section are tasty, but none are particularly 'salty' and only the curries 'spicy'.

Pesto Tartlets
Stilton and Leek Tartlets
Stuffed Peppers
Roasted Vegetables with Halloumi on a bed of Couscous
Gnocchi with Blue Cheese and Broccoli
Frittata
Pasta with Home-made Tomato Sauce
Pizza
Chicken Curry
Vegetable Curry
Dutch Stamppot aka Sausages with Endives/Kale and Potato Mash
Vegetarian Dutch Stamppot

PESTO TARTLETS

A tartlet is simply a mini tart, just like a piglet is a baby pig, the suffix 'let' meaning 'smaller' or 'lesser'. In this recipe I prefer to make mini tarts, hence 'tartlet' as you can vary the toppings to meet every-one's tastes, in a large family, this is quite important, and they can be easily served at parties as bite-size nibbles.

Ingredients
1 pack of ready-made puff pastry
4-5 tbsp pesto, (I use a selection of red and green pesto,
see Chapter 8 for green pesto recipe)
Handful of olives, roasted peppers, sun-dried tomatoes or sweetcorn
Cheese selection: Cheddar, mozzarella, halloumi or goat's cheese
Meat selection: chorizo, pepperoni, ham (optional)

Method
Roll out the pastry into squares roughly 3" by 3" / 7½ cm by 7½ cm, spread a thin covering of pesto, add 3-4 olives, peppers, sweetcorn or sun-dried tomatoes, and meat if required, cover with cheese of choice.

Place on a baking tray on top of the woodburner, although the pastry won't puff up quite as much as when cooked in the oven, the overall taste will be just as good.

STILTON AND LEEK TARTLETS

There is historical evidence to suggest that Stilton cheese has been made and sold in the vicinity of the village of Stilton in Cambridgeshire since the late 17th Century, however the cheese was not invented by one particular person, it evolved over time from a creamy cheese, to the blue veined cheese we know today.

Ingredients
25g/1oz butter/margarine
1 large leek, trimmed and sliced
½ tsp ground nutmeg
1 pack of ready-made puff pastry
3 ½ oz/100g Stilton
1 free-range egg

Method
Lightly fry the leek on the woodburner in the butter or margarine, add the nutmeg. Roll out the pastry and cut into circles, either a large mug or saucer size, to fit on a side plate, cover the pastry with the leeks, add crumbled Stilton on top and brush the edges of the pastry with beaten egg. Place on a baking sheet on top of the woodburner, until cooked.

STUFFED PEPPERS

The origins of the humble stuffed pepper is hard to ascertain as no one country can claim to be the founder of this tasty dish. Variations can be found across the globe. In Europe, namely Spain, Greece, Germany and Hungary have their own variants, but so do the Middle East, India, North Africa, Mexico, Guatemala, the Scandinavian and Baltic countries as well as the United States. What this tells us that this is a very flexible dish, with the main theme being a bell pepper stuffed with either meat, rice, or vegetables, often topped with cheese, the adaptations, simply suit the tastes of the local inhabitants.

Ingredients
Selection of red, green, yellow bell peppers
Filling 1
Minced meat or soya mince
1 onion, finely chopped
1 clove garlic, crushed
½ courgette, chopped
½ aubergine, chopped
3 tbsp passata
1 tbsp extra virgi olive oil
Filling 2
Handful of cooked rice
½ courgette, chopped
1 onion, finely chopped
1 clove garlic, crushed
½ red, green, yellow bell peppers, chopped
½ aubergine, chopped
1 tbsp extra virgin olive oil
For the topping
Cheese selection: Cheddar, mozzarella or halloumi

Method
Cut the peppers in half, lengthways and scoop out the seeds.

For **filling 1**, fry the onion, garlic, courgettes and aubergine on the woodburner in the olive oil, separately fry the mincemeat and add to the vegetable mix, with plenty of passata. Alternatively if you are using soya mince, fry the vegetables first and add the soya mince to the vegetable mix at the same time as adding the passata. Leave to cook on the woodburner.

For **filling 2**, fry the onion, garlic, courgettes, aubergine and any peppers not used as shells for filling, in the olive oil. In a separate pan, boil rice on the woodburner. Mix all the ingredients together.

Fill the pepper shells with your choice of filling, cover with cheese of choice and place in a baking sheet on the woodburner to cook. Serve with a fresh, green salad.

Roasted Vegetables with Halloumi on a bed of Couscous

Halloumi comes from the Greek island of Cyprus and is a soft curd-like cheese that is made from sheep's milk, unlike many cheeses it doesn't contain rennet, therefore is suitable for vegetarians, but not vegans. Halloumi is best eaten cooked, as opposed to raw.

Ingredients

This dish can either be used as a vegetable accompaniment to a meat dish, or as a light lunch in its own right, simply add warm pitta bread and houmous.

½ aubergine, chopped
½ courgette, chopped
4-5 tomatoes, chopped
¼ red, green, yellow bell peppers, chopped
½ pack of halloumi
Drizzle of extra virgin olive oil
Couscous
1 stock cube /pot (optional)

Method

Chop the vegetables and halloumi into bite sized pieces place on a small baking tray and drizzle with olive oil, place on top of the wood-burner, and turn regularly until cooked.

For the couscous, boil water on the woodburner, either in a kettle or saucepan, pour over the couscous. If you are using a flavoured couscous, then the couscous is ready to serve, if using plain, add a stock cube/pot to the boiling water, to flavour the couscous.

Once the roasted vegetables and halloumi are ready, pour over the couscous and if you are eating this dish as a meal, serve with warm pitta bread, simply place the pitta bread on the top of the wood-burner, whilst the vegetables and halloumi are cooking, and turn regularly, add a dollop of houmous, see Chapter 8, for a truly tasty treat.

GNOCCHI WITH BLUE CHEESE AND BROCCOLI

Gnocchi are small potato dumplings, but if you look back in history, gnocchi may be the ancestor to what we know today as pasta. In *The Encyclopedia of Pasta* by Oretta Zanini De Vita, you will see that gnocchi is referred to as 'primal pasta'. Originally gnocchi was made with flour, then by the early 19th Century, with the emergence of potato, one part potato was used to make gnocchi, still using 3 parts flour. It was not until the 20th Century that potato became the main ingredient in gnocchi, with flour only used to bind it together.

Ingredients
1 pack of gnocchi
1 pack of blue cheese: Stilton, Saint Agur, Gorgonzola
½ pack soft cream cheese
1 broccoli, trimmed

Method
Cook the gnocchi in a pan of boiling water on the woodburner, if you have a bamboo steamer, you can steam the broccoli at the same time over the gnocchi, if not cook separately. In another pan, melt the blue cheese and soft cheese together. Once the cheese has melted and the other ingredients are ready, mix together and serve with a salad.

Frittata

The name 'frittata' comes from the Italian 'to fry'. However, despite the frittata being a quintessentially Italian dish, you won't find it in many Italian recipe books as it is simply a home-cooked dish, utilising leftovers. Similar to the humble omelette, which has extra ingredients added to it whilst cooking, then is served folded, in a frittata the eggs are mixed with the other ingredients from the start, and cooked together slowly, a frittata is slightly thicker than an omelette, and is therefore not folded before being served.

Ingredients

Dozen or so new potatoes, sliced
½ red, green, yellow bell peppers, chopped
½ courgette, chopped
1 red onion, finely chopped
Handful of chorizo, sliced
2 tbsp extra virgin olive oil
6 medium free-range eggs
1 dash of milk

Method

Boil the new potatoes in a pan on the woodburner, when the potatoes are nearly cooked, take them off the heat. Fry the vegetables together in 1 tbsp of the olive oil in another pan. Mix the eggs with a dash of milk, and heat the remaining olive oil in a frying pan, when hot, add the egg mixture, vegetables, including the potatoes, and chorizo and cook all together.

PASTA WITH HOME-MADE TOMATO SAUCE

For many of us, pasta with tomato sauce is a quintessentially Italian dish which epitomises Italian cooking, however, interestingly, tomatoes didn't become part of the Italian diet until the 1800s and the first known recipe for pasta with tomato sauce can be found in the 1790 cookbook *L'Apicio Moderno* by Francesco Leornardi. This sauce, in Italian 'marinara', is often the cornerstone for many other Italian pasta sauces such as 'arrabbiata' which is a spicier version with chilli added. The true marinara sauce simply consist of olive oil, garlic, tomatoes and herbs, with only sometimes the addition of onion. I have adapted the original recipe by adding extra ingredients, hence simply referring to it as 'tomato sauce' rather than the more purist 'marinara'.

Ingredients

Pasta of choice (approximately 2oz, 50g per person)
1 red onion, finely chopped
½ aubergine, chopped
½ courgette, chopped
1 clove garlic, crushed
1 tin chopped tomatoes/passata
2 tbsp tomato purée
1 pinch of Italian herbs or mixed dried herbs
1 pack of mozzarella
1 tbsp extra virgin olive oil
Handful of Parmesan or Cheddar cheese

Method

Cook the pasta in boiling water until al dente, and fry the vegetables in the olive oil on the woodburner, when soft, add the herbs, tomato purée, passata and or tinned tomatoes, and leave to simmer. Under normal circumstances I blend the pasta sauce before serving, a great way to get younger children to eat a variety of vegetables, if you have no power, I would suggest chopping the vegetables as small as possible, if not grating them, to prevent picky eaters removing anything remotely healthy looking. Pour the pasta sauce over the cooked pasta, and add chopped mozzarella just before serving, so it has a chance to melt, sprinkle with grated Parmesan or Cheddar cheese.

PIZZA

The beauty about making pizza is it is very hands on, even with the younger members of the family. My children have grown up helping me in the kitchen, and after cake making, this is one of their favourite meals to prepare. Rolling the dough is pretty much like playing with playdough, just less colourful, and spreading the passata and adding toppings is always a favourite, particularly when there is spare mozzarella and olives to munch on! The only downside of home-made pizza is the mess, even when the kids aren't involved the kitchen looks slightly worse for wear afterwards, with flour on the floor, and myself, and sticky dough on the worktop, however, the smell and ultimate taste of home-made, wood-fired pizza overcomes any slight domestic cleaning issues.

Ingredients
For the pizza dough
10fl oz/275ml water
2 tbsp extra virgin olive oil
2 tsp salt
2 tsp sugar
1lb/450g of strong white bread flour
2 ½ tsp instant yeast
For the toppings
½ tin chopped tomatoes/passata
1 pinch of Italian herbs or mixed dried herbs
Vegetable selection: onion, red, green or yellow bell peppers, mushrooms, sweetcorn, olives, sun-dried tomatoes, chopped
1 pack of mozzarella, and a sprinkling of Parmesan and or Cheddar cheese
Meat selection: chorizo, pepperoni, ham
Drizzle of extra virgin olive oil

Method
Either add all of the above pizza dough ingredients to the breadmaker in the order listed, or add to a bowl and mix, then leave to rise with a tea towel over the bowl. Once risen, knead the dough, even if the breadmaker has done the hard work for you, then roll out to the size of pizza required, ideally to fit your pizza stone, if you have one, alternatively place on a lightly oiled baking sheet.

Once the pizza dough is ready, cover with passata or chopped tomatoes and add a sprinkling of herbs. Then chop and decorate with your vegetables of choice, add meat as required, then chopped mozzarella, and a sprinkling of either grated Parmesan or Cheddar cheese, drizzle with olive oil before cooking.

CHICKEN CURRY

Traditionally, in the UK, the word 'curry' was used to describe any dish that has a sauce flavoured with curry powder. Today with the popularity of cookery programmes, and the availability of fresh spices such as ginger, garlic, turmeric, coriander, cumin, cinnamon, cardamom and cayenne, these are often used as opposed to the generic curry powder. The first recipe for 'curry' that was published in the UK, was by Hannah Glasse in 1747, in her book entitled *The Art of Cookery made Plain and Easy*. Many curry recipes can be found in late 19th Century cookery books, such as Mrs Beeton's *Every Day Cookery and Housekeeping Book*, surely a classic of all time, Mrs Beeton actually has a recipe for curry powder which includes, turmeric, cumin, coriander black pepper, cayenne pepper, ginger, caraway seeds and cardamoms.

Ingredients
½ whole cooked chicken
1 sweet potato, chopped
1 carrot, chopped
Handful of peas/sweetcorn
½ tin coconut milk
1 pinch of Indian/Indonesian spices (see above)
2 tbsp extra virgin olive oil

Method
Parboil the sweet potato and carrot, then fry them in the olive oil, stirring regularly, remove the meat from the chicken and add to the pan, add sweetcorn and or peas, and the spices, once the spices have been thoroughly stirred in, add the coconut milk and leave to simmer so the flavours have a chance to infuse the meat and vegetables. Serve with home-made Indian flatbread, see Chapter 5.

VEGETABLE CURRY

It is a common held belief that most Indians are vegetarian, this is not so. In fact approximately 70 per cent of Indians actually eat meat. One of the reasons this misconception arose, is because different castes often favour different meats, so by providing a truly vegetarian meal at public banquets and ceremonies, this ensured that everyone could eat and no one would be offended by the menu.

If you would like to add more protein to this dish, you can add either chickpeas, for a truly vegetarian dish, or cooked prawns, if not. Please note, if you are cooking on the woodburner alone, I would ensure you add cooked prawns, as opposed to the uncooked variety.

Ingredients
1 sweet potato, chopped
1 carrot, chopped
½ aubergine, chopped
Handful of mushrooms, sliced
½ courgette, chopped
Handful of peas/sweetcorn
1 pinch of Indian/Indonesian spices
½ tin coconut milk
½ tin chickpeas (optional)
2 tbsp extra virgin olive oil
1 pack of cooked prawns (very optional, and
not to be recommended if you are truly vegetarian)

Method
Parboil the sweet potato and carrot, then place the rest of the chopped vegetables in a pan on the woodburner with the olive oil, when they start to soften, add the sweet potato, carrot and sweetcorn and or peas, it is at this point that you would add protein in the form of chickpeas or prawns, then add the spices, once the spices have been thoroughly stirred in, add the coconut milk and leave to simmer so the flavours have a chance to infuse the vegetables. Serve with home-made Indian flatbread, see Chapter 5.

DUTCH STAMPPOT AKA SAUSAGES WITH ENDIVES/KALE AND POTATO MASH

Married to a Dutchman, I had to include at least one traditionally Dutch recipe in my book, and this is one of our favourites, it is very much a Winter warmer, a quintessentially Dutch dish to be served in the Winter months. I have even developed a vegetarian alternative, for myself.

Ingredients
1lb/450g potatoes, chopped
7oz/200g endives (to be traditionally Dutch), kale, or I sometimes use spinach instead
¾ pack of bacon
2 Dutch Rookworst sausages per person, or any smoked sausage
1 dash of milk
1 knob of butter/margarine
2 tbsp extra virgin olive oil
½ pint of gravy (optional)

Method
Bring the potatoes to the boil on the woodburner, then simmer until cooked. Mash with butter or margarine and milk, add the endives, kale or spinach. Fry the bacon in a frying pan with the olive oil and add to the potato and vegetable mix. Cook the sausages in the olive oil on the woodburner and place on top of the mashed potato. Serve with gravy, if you wish.

VEGETARIAN DUTCH STAMPPOT

Although vegetarianism has been popular in the UK since the end of World War 2, in the Netherlands, vegetarianism is a newer phenomenon. The Dutch vegetarian population has certainly increased in the last 15 years, however, there are still very few vegans in Holland in fact only 0·4 per cent of the population, compared to over 1 per cent in the UK. Obviously the following dish is not vegan, using goat's cheese as an alternative to bacon.

Ingredients
1lb/450g potatoes, chopped
7oz/200g endives (to be traditionally Dutch), kale, or I sometimes use spinach instead
3-4 slices goat's cheese
2 vegetarian sausages, per person
1 dash of milk
1 knob of butter/margarine
1 tbsp extra virgin olive oil
½ pint of vegetarian gravy (optional)

Method
Prepare the potatoes as per the meat version, replacing the bacon with goat's cheese. Cook the vegetarian sausages in the olive oil and serve on top of the mashed potato. Serve with vegetarian gravy, if you wish.

CHAPTER 5
ACCOMPANIMENTS

The word 'accompaniment' became part of the English language in the 18th Century, but was originally used to describe a part in a song that acts as background to the main piece. It was only later that the word became commonly used to describe something that compliments something else making the whole thing better. For example when referring to food, an accompaniment is a secondary dish, although not essential to the meal, once added, makes the meal more satisfying. The following accompaniments can not necessarily be cooked on a woodburner, in fact coleslaw is not a cooked dish at all.

Home-made Bread Rolls
Parmesan and Sun-dried Tomato Rolls
Garlic Bread
Indian Flatbread
Coleslaw
Sauté Potatoes
Ratatouille

HOME-MADE BREAD ROLLS

Bread has been around in a variety of forms for at least 30,000 years, one of the reasons it is the most widely eaten food in the world, is because it is easily portable, unlike other carbohydrates such as rice and pasta.

If you have a complete power failure, you will need to make bread from scratch, and the recipe is below. However, I was lucky enough to have a power supply in some parts of the house, just not all of the kitchen, so was able to use my breadmaker to prepare the bread, but either way ingredients and process is the same.

Ingredients
10fl oz/275ml of water
2 tbsp extra virgin olive oil
2 tsp salt
2 tsp sugar
16oz/450g of strong bread flour (either wholemeal or white)
2 ½ tsp yeast

Method
If you have a breadmaker and power, then all ingredients go into the breadmaker in the order listed, order is important, and you turn onto dough cycle.

If you don't have a breadmaker, or the power to use one, mix the ingredients together by hand, in the order listed, knead, and leave to rest in a warm place with a clean, dry tea towel over the top for at least 1 hour.

Once the dough is proven, knead for a further couple of minutes, then shape into roll sizes, place on a greased, lined baking sheet, and put on top of the woodburner to cook, you will need to turn the rolls regularly. The smell of the warm bread alone is enough to make you hungry, and can be eaten as an accompaniment to any meal, but goes particularly well with home-made soup.

Parmesan and Sun-dried Tomato Rolls

Parmesan, as it is often referred to in English, or Parmigiano Reggiano to give it is correct, Italian name, is a hard cheese, which dates back to the 13th Century where it was originally produced in two Italian regions, Parma and Reggio Emilia. It wasn't until 1934 that the two regions standardized their cheeses, to make what is now Parmigiano Reggiano, or Parmesan cheese.

Ingredients
9fl oz/250ml water
1fl oz/25ml extra virgin olive oil
1 tbsp sugar
2 tsp salt
16oz/440g of strong white bread flour
1 ¼oz/30g Parmesan
1 ¼ tsp instant dried yeast
2oz/50g sun-dried tomatoes (add once the dough has risen)
1 tbsp sun-dried tomato oil (the oil that is in the sun-dried tomato jar)
/extra virgin olive oil

Method
Either add the ingredients to the breadmaker, in the order listed, alternatively add the ingredients to a bowl, in the order listed above, and mix together by hand, once mixed knead until resembling a dough consistency, then cover and leave to rise. Add the sun-dried tomatoes after the dough has risen, then shape into rolls and place on a greased baking sheet. I prefer to use sun-dried tomato oil, but equally olive oil can be used. Bake on top of the woodburner, remembering to turn regularly as the heat is direct not convection as per an oven. If you are cooking conventionally just bake in the oven at approximately 180C for 20 minutes.

GARLIC BREAD

'Italian garlic bread' is more of an American invention than a truly Italian one. In Italy, bruschetta, which is crusty bread, with finely chopped tomatoes, fresh basil, roasted peppers and prosciutto ham on top, was originally simply lightly toasted crusty bread with crushed garlic and olive oil, and it is this basic bruschetta that the American garlic bread originated from. When Italian immigrants came to America, they often had to make do with local ingredients, instead of olive oil, they used butter which was readily available, and garlic bread as we know it today was born.

Ingredients
1 French stick/baguette
1-2 cloves of garlic
2 knobs of butter/margarine

Method

Cut the baguette lengthways, then slice half-way through the bread, widthways, roughly the size of a portion. Crush the garlic and mix with the butter or margarine, then simply spread along the cut bread, ie both lengthways and widthways to ensure an even covering. Wrap the bread in silver foil, and bake in the oven at approximately 180C for 20 minutes, or until the bread is slightly crispy, and all the butter melted. Cut along the widthway slits, and serve. This is not a wood-burner recipe but a good accompaniment to serve with soup or any Italian dish.

INDIAN FLATBREAD

There are over 30 Indian flatbreads, all reflecting the different regions, ingredients and cooking methods used. The most famous being naan, chapati and paratha, to name just a few. However, what all these flatbreads have in common is their use, they are excellent at mopping up the curries they are usually served as an accompaniment to.

I have used the generic term 'Indian flatbread', as I don't claim to be an expert on this matter.

Ingredients
11fl oz/300ml water
2tbsp extra virgin olive oil
1 tsp salt
1 tsp sugar
16oz/450g of strong white bread flour
2 tsp instant yeast
Egg wash (1 free-range egg, 1 tbsp water,1 pinch of salt)

Method
Place all of the ingredients in the breadmaker, in the order listed, if you are using a breadmaker and turn to the dough cycle, or mix by hand, in the order listed, if not. Once the mixture resembles a dough-like consistency, leave to rise for a couple of hours, with a clean tea towel covering the bowl.

Whether preparing by hand, or not, knead the dough on a floured surface, and shape into small balls roughly the size of an orange, then roll out so the circles become more or less the size of a saucer. Place on a lightly greased pizza stone or baking sheet on the woodburner, watching and turning regularly, serve with your choice of curry, see Chapter 4.

COLESLAW

The word 'coleslaw' comes from the Dutch word 'koolsla' meaning cabbage salad. The 'kool' part of the word is the Dutch for 'cabbage' and the 'sla' is an abbreviation of the Dutch word for 'salade'. Back in the late 17th Century, many Dutch settlers moved to New York, in fact for a while the city was known as New Amsterdam. The Dutch brought their cabbage salad with them, and it soon became a popular American accompaniment to many meals.

Ingredients
¼ of white cabbage, finely chopped
1 carrot, grated
½ white onion, peeled and grated, or 2 spring onions, chopped
½ apple, grated (optional)
2-3 tbsp mayonnaise or Frittesaus (to be truly Dutch)

Method
Finely chop the cabbage, grate the carrot (and apple if you wish), and add to the cabbage, either grate the white onion, or finely chop the spring onions and add to the mix, stir in mayonnaise to taste. Although coleslaw is not a woodburner recipe, it makes a good vegetable accompaniment when cooking resourses are limited.

SAUTÉ POTATOES

The word 'sauté' is a French word, which translated simply means 'to jump', this method of cooking utilises a shallow pan such as a frying pan, but with a very small amount of fat and the food is tossed around whilst cooking. I prefer to use either extra virgin olive oil, or sun-dried tomato oil, which gives a slightly sweet flavour to the potatoes.

Ingredients

1½lb/700g potatoes, preferably Charlotte or other new/baby potatoes
2-3 tbsp sun-dried tomato oil (the oil that is in the sun-dried tomato jar)
/extra virgin olive oil
Spices, garlic salt or if you are travelling to Holland I recommend the brand
Verstegen mix voor Aardappel (Aardappel
simply being the Dutch word for potato)

Method

Slice, but do not peel the potatoes, then parboil in a pan on the wood-burner, when they are al dente, drain and heat the oil in a frying pan on the woodburner, add the potatoes and spices and stir regularly so the potatoes are tossed in the oil and spices to prevent sticking.

Ratatouille

Another French dish, this time originating in the area around Provence and Nice in the late 18th Century. At first ratatouille was a peasant's dish, and was prepared with courgettes, tomatoes, green and red peppers, onions and garlic, but today aubergine is usually added as well. Nowadays ratatouille tends to be an accompaniment to the main meal, but can be served as a vegetarian dish in its own right.

Ingredients

1 onion, white or red, finely chopped
½ courgette, chopped
½ aubergine, chopped
1 clove of garlic, crushed
¼ red, green or yellow bell pepper, chopped
1 tin of tomatoes
3 tbsp passata
1 pinch of herbs from Provence or mixed dried herbs
1 tbsp extra virgin olive oil
½ pack of mozzarella and or Cheddar cheese

Method

Chop all the vegetables, lightly fry on the woodburner in the olive oil, once the vegetables are soft, add herbs, tomatoes and passata and leave to simmer. Although not traditional, I like to add either small pieces of mozzarella cheese or grated Cheddar cheese to the ratatouille before serving. Place the ratatouille in an oven-proof dish and sprinkle the cheese on top, if cooking conventionally, place in the oven at 180C for 10 minutes. If cooking on the woodburner, put the oven-proof dish on top of the woodburner for 10 minutes, the cheese will still melt, it just won't brown.

CHAPTER 6
PUDDINGS

What is the difference between a pudding and a dessert? Is it all in the old English class system where according to *Debrett's*, the answer is "pudding, never 'sweet', 'afters' or 'dessert' (except when describing a fruit course)". However it is not that simple, it also has to do with the dish itself, whereas a pudding can be sweet or savoury, eg black pudding, steak and kidney pudding, Yorkshire pudding, a dessert is always sweet. In addition a pudding is usually considered more rustic, such as 'spotted dick', 'jam roly poly', 'Christmas pudding' whereas a dessert is lighter, not always cooked such as a jelly or mousse. For the purpose of this book, I will refer to the sweet course of the meal as pudding, simply because this is the word I grew up with.

My husband and our French student are particularly keen on puddings, so as well as making a variety of non-cooked puddings, I experimented with cooking puddings utilising the woodburner, in some recipes the woodburner was only used to melt a couple of ingredients, in others it was used to cook the dish in its entirety.

Jam Roly Poly
Chocolate Biscuit Cake aka Refrigerator Cake
Rocky Road
Welsh Cakes

Jam Roly Poly

Traditionally jam roly poly is a pudding made from suet dough, spread with jam, rolled up and either boiled or steamed. It was first created in the 19th Century, and was also known as 'shirt-sleeve pudding' as it was often steamed in an old shirt-sleeve. However, one definition of 'roly poly' according to James Orchard Halliwell-Phillips in his book, *A Dictionary of Archaic and Provincial Words from the Fourteenth Century*, is "a pudding made in round layers, with preserves or treacle between". It is this definition that I believe makes my puff pastry version still deserving of the name, despite not being made of suet.

Ingredients
1 pack of ready-made puff pastry
Jam, whichever flavour you prefer, or have in the fridge!

Method
Simply roll out the puff pastry and spread with a thin covering of jam, roll back up and place on greaseproof paper, in a baking tray on top of the woodburner.

When ready, slice the jam roly poly into portions and serve with Greek yoghurt, cream, vanilla ice cream, or if you have ready-made custard, this can also be warmed on the woodburner.

CHOCOLATE BISCUIT CAKE AKA REFRIGERATOR CAKE

If you are without power to your fridge, I suggest you make this recipe in the Winter months only, and store outside in an airtight container. Although this is a non-cook cake, ie you don't need an oven to bake it, you do need heat to melt the butter and syrup hence classing it as a woodburner recipe. In fact during our 3 week stint without power, my husband celebrated his birthday, without thinking I asked him what cake he would like, and afterwards remembered that baking was a problem, fortunately for me he asked for a chocolate cake, hence the following recipe was used to make a birthday cake, with the addition of candles and a selection of berries, it still made a tasty celebratory cake.

Ingredients
4oz/110g butter/margarine
2oz/50g sugar
2 tbsp cocoa
2oz/50g raisins or other dried fruit
¼ tsp vanilla essence (see Chapter 8 for home-made vanilla essence)
2 tbsp golden syrup
8oz/225g biscuits, preferably digestives, (if your biscuit tin is anything like mine, use up all your broken biscuits when making this dish)
2oz/50g nuts (optional)

Method
Melt butter or margarine, sugar, cocoa and syrup in a pan on the woodburner, crush the biscuits with a rolling pin, I prefer to use the end of the rolling pin in a large mixing bowl to get the pestle and mortar effect, but on a larger scale. Add the crushed biscuits, raisins or dried fruit and nuts if you wish, as well as the vanilla essence. Place in a lightly greased cake tin, grease with the butter or margarine used in the recipe rather than oil, and chill either in the fridge if it has power, or in the garden if not. Please note, if you are without power and it is 30C outside, this is not a good recipe!

ROCKY ROAD

'Rocky Road' was invented in Australia back in 1853, as a way to sell confectionery that had become damaged on the long journey from Europe, with the aid of locally foraged nuts and cheap chocolate the damaged sweets were made into this tasty treat, the name originating from the 'Rocky Road' that the travellers had to take to get to the gold fields.

Ingredients

7oz/200g cooking chocolate
2-3tbsp golden syrup
4 ¾oz/135g butter/margarine
3 ½oz/100g mini marshmallows
7oz/200g digestive biscuits
Handful of raisins/dried cranberries/nuts (optional)

Method

Line a baking tray with greaseproof paper, crush biscuits, as per chocolate biscuit cake recipe, melt butter or margarine, chocolate and syrup in a pan on the woodburner. Mix all the ingredients together and place in the baking tray, preferably chill before serving, again in the fridge if you have power, or outside in an airtight container during the Winter months.

WELSH CAKES

Welsh cakes, otherwise known as bakestones in Wales, have been popular since the later 19th Century. Traditionally cooked on a bakestone or griddle, I have adapted the recipe for the woodburner.

Ingredients
1lb 2oz/500g self raising flour
3oz/75g sugar
1 heaped tsp spice: allspice or mixed spice
9oz/250g butter/margarine
1 pinch of salt
5oz/150g dried fruit, raisins, sultanas, cranberries
1 large free-range egg
2 dashes of milk
Serve with butter/margarine and jam

Method
Sieve the flour, add sugar and spice, cut the butter or margarine into small pieces then using your fingertips, rub into the dry ingredients until it resembles breadcrumbs, add the dried fruit, make a well in the centre and break in the egg. Add a couple of dashes of milk, start with just a little, you can always add more, but can't take it away if you add too much. Then using a fork, mix the dough together, once roughly mixed with the fork, this is the fun bit, with clean hands pat the dough into shape, it is easier if you do small quantities at a time. Then roll out to approximately ½"/1cm thick circles and using a pastry cutter or cup, I prefer a cup, cut the dough into Welsh cakes. If you have a skillet, use this to cook the Welsh cakes on the woodburner, if not, improvise. I heated the pizza stone on the woodburner, when it was warm I very lightly buttered my pizza stone, with the same butter or margarine used in the recipe, then placed half a dozen Welsh cakes on top, turn regularly, until they are lightly golden on each side. Serve buttered with your favourite jam on top. I prefer to eat the Welsh cakes straight from the woodburner whilst warm, a very yummy treat on a cold Winter's day.

CHAPTER 7
FESTIVE RECIPES

I have focused on Christmas and Halloween for the purpose of this book. To me, Easter is of equal importance to Christmas, but not always cold enough to require the woodburner.

Part I – Christmas

One Christmas our entire village was without power on the night before Christmas Eve, we cooked pizzas on the woodburner, mulled wine and ate by candlelight, it was very cosy and romantic. The following day, family started to arrive, a starter of home-made soup made on the woodburner, followed by cold pre-cooked salmon and jacket potatoes cooked on the woodburner gave us a festive but warm lunch. That evening we went to church for the Christmas Eve service. We sang by candlelight in the church and watched our children perform the nativity, the bonhomie amongst the congregation was even greater than normal. As we left the church and returned to our homes, the power came back on, almost as if the whole village coming together to celebrate the festivities despite the lack of power, worked a miracle. Christmas resumed as previous years, the worries of how to store, let alone cook our turkeys over, but I am convinced that even if the power had not come back on, we would still have had a very happy Christmas. Christmas should be a time of coming together, whether friends, family or neighbours, and helping one another is surely the best gift we can give.

Mulled Wine
Mincemeat Roly Poly
Chocolate Truffles
Roasted Chestnuts (See Chapter 9 Foraging)
Popcorn

MULLED WINE

It's not Christmas without mulled wine, or gluewein as it is known in Germany, a traditional Winter warmer, with a hint of festive aromas. Over the years I have adapted the recipe to make an easy, but equally tasty version. The beginning of December is a good time to make the first mulled wine, to drink whilst decorating the Christmas tree.

Ingredients
1 bottle of cheap red wine
A couple of dashes of orange juice
2-3 tbsp sugar
1 pinch of spices: allspice, mixed spice, cloves
1 dash of spirit, ie brandy, whisky, rum (whatever you have available)

Method
In a large saucepan on the woodburner add the wine, spirits, juice, sugar and spices, simply heat and stir until all the sugar is dissolved, and the wine is quite warm, but not boiling, serve with Christmas music playing in the background. If you like your mulled wine more alcoholic, simply add more than one dash of spirits to the mix; as mulled wine is quite a moreish drink, I favour lots of orange juice and only a small dash of spirit, if any at all, so you can drink more! If you have a sweet tooth, add more sugar, this is one recipe where you can really experiment with. But please note, if you do add cloves to give that truly Christmassy aroma, remove them with a sieve or tea strainer before serving.

MINCEMEAT ROLY POLY

Mincemeat is a mixture of chopped dried fruit, spices and spirits, (the alcoholic variety, this is a Christmas dish not Halloween) with suet added. Originally all mincemeat contained meat in the form of beef suet, hence the name, so not very vegetarian friendly, but today many commercial mincemeats use vegetable shortening instead.

If you haven't had the time or inclination to prepare the mince pies in advance, this is an equally tasty dish, which still gives that Christmassy aroma to the house.

Ingredients
1 pack of ready-made puff pastry
Half a jar of mincemeat

Method
Simply roll out the puff pastry and spread with a thin covering of mincemeat, roll back up and place on greaseproof paper, in a baking tray on top of the woodburner.

When ready, slice the mincemeat roly poly into portions and serve with Greek yoghurt, cream, vanilla ice cream, or if you have ready-made custard, this can also be warmed in a pan on the woodburner.

CHOCOLATE TRUFFLES

Once again, as with many of our culinary delights, we have the French to thank for this delicious treat. The original chocolate truffle resembled the black truffle mushroom which can be found exclusively in Southern Europe, hence the name. Truffles were originally just chocolate and cream rolled in cocoa, sometimes with a flavouring added. But according to legend, the first ever chocolate truffle was made accidentally in the 1920s when a French apprentice unintentionally added hot cream to a bowl of chocolate. As the mixture hardened, he shaped it into a ball and rolled it in cocoa, and 'voilà' the truffle was born.

Ingredients
10 ½fl oz/300ml double cream
1 knob of butter/margarine
Grated zest of 1 clementine
10 ½oz/300g of 70% dark chocolate broken into pieces
1 pinch of salt
1 dash of brandy
Suggestions for coating the truffles
Handful of mixed chopped nuts
3 tbsp cocoa powder
3 tbsp shredded coconut
3 tbsp chocolate vermicelli

Method

Heat the cream in a pan on the woodburner, do not boil, add butter or margarine and clementine zest.

Once the butter or margarine has melted, pour the mixture over the chocolate, whisking gently. Add salt, stir in brandy and shape into balls, then put in the fridge to set for a couple of hours, assuming your fridge has power.

After roughly two hours, take the chocolate mixture out of the fridge to warm up, prepare bowls of nuts, coconut, cocoa and chocolate vermicelli, obviously you can just use one, two, three or all four coatings, depending on your taste and what is available at the time. Then roll the chocolate balls in the various coatings and serve, either on a plate, or in mini paper cup cake cases, or in tiny boxes if giving as gifts. These do make wonderful Christmas presents for teachers, friends and family, alternatively children and grandparents alike enjoy choosing their own coatings, and rolling the truffles themselves, be warned though, this can get quite messy!

POPCORN

Since the 1500s, the Aztec Indians have used popcorn in their ceremonies, as garlands, they even performed a popcorn dance, and in Mexico, remnants of popcorn have been found that date back to approximately 3600BC. Popcorn is still used as a decoration on Christmas trees, and artificial popcorn can be bought for this purpose, but traditionally popcorn, along with fruit such as cranberries, was made into garlands to adorn the tree, before commercial decorations were readily available. Today popcorn is associated with the cinema, and is usually eaten salted or sweetened. I'm afraid I'm not a great fan of eating popcorn, but I am a fan of making it, especially with kids.

Ingredients
1 bag of popcorn
2-3 tbsp sunflower oil
Sugar or salt to taste

Method
Place the popcorn into some hot oil in the bottom of a cast iron pan on the woodburner, stir well and put the lid on as soon as it starts to pop. Either eat as it is, or add sugar or salt to taste.

CHAPTER 7
FESTIVE RECIPES

Part II – Halloween

Halloween is celebrated on 31st October, the day before All Saints Day or All Hallows Day as it is otherwise known, which is on 1st November. All Hallows Eve over the years became known as Halloween. Halloween is based on a Celtic tradition when people would light bonfires and wear costumes to ward off ghosts. Today Halloween is celebrated with Halloween parties, where children dress up in spooky costumes, carve pumpkins into jack o' lanterns, play games such as apple bobbing, and visit friends and neighbours 'trick or treating'.

I have held a Halloween party for the past 14 years, and making Halloween food is always rather fun, and gruesome, some dishes more appetising than others!

Devilled Eyeballs
Hot Dog Fingers
Pumpkin Soup
Toasted Marshmallows aka S'mores

DEVILLED EYEBALLS

Which came first, the chicken or the egg? This classic dilemma is based on the fact that all chickens hatch from eggs, and that all chicken eggs are laid by chickens.

Based on Darwin's theory of evolution, the answer would be that chickens had ancestors that weren't chickens, and therefore the egg came first, as it was laid by a bird that was not a chicken.

Ingredients
Free-range eggs (each egg makes two eyeballs)
Olives (½ olive per ½ egg)
1 tbsp mayonnaise
1 pinch of paprika
Drizzle of red food colouring

Method
Hardboil as many eggs as you wish on the woodburner, but please remember this dish is not appetising, I made a whole plateful last year, and even I struggled to eat them despite knowing and liking all of the ingredients. This year I made a token two, basically one egg cut in half, as they do make a fantastic table decoration.

Hardboil the egg or eggs, peel and cut in half lengthways. Scoop out the yolk and mix with mayonnaise and a little paprika to flavour, put the yolk mixture back in the egg and place half an olive on top. With the red food colouring, drizzle a little from the yolk to the edge of the white of the egg, to resemble blood, you won't need to use your imagination, it really does resemble blood!

HOT DOG FINGERS

Hot dogs are synonymous with America and American baseball in particular. In general, hot dogs are far more processed than the German bratwurst. The bratwurst dates back to the early 1300s in Nuremburg, Germany. German immigrants brought their sausage recipe to America, where it became popular in the 1920s in Wisconsin. The hot dog also originated in Germany, but this time from the city of Frankfurt, hence the name Frankfurter, dating back to 1487, and arrived in America in 1860s. Bratwursts tend to be fresher, less processed than hot dogs, and hot dogs tend to contain far more sodium and preservatives than bratwursts, however, it is important to remember that bratwursts are generally bigger than the humble hot dog, and this needs to be taken into account, when evaluating the health benefits of one over the other.

Ingredients
1 jar of hot dog sausages or bratwurst
1 pack of finger rolls (excuse the pun)
1 knob butter/margarine (optional)
Drizzle of tomato ketchup (optional)

Method
Peel the top layer of skin off the hot dog sausages, in the shape of a finger nail, carve a couple of horizontal lines halfway down to resemble knuckles. Cook the hot dog sausages in a pan on the wood-burner, when cooked place in the rolls, buttered if you prefer, serve with ketchup for that spooky bloodied finger effect.

Pumpkin Soup

I have included this in the Halloween section, but equally it could have been included in the Soup section. This is rather a waste not want not recipe, in that as the children carve their pumpkins each year, I hover in the background rescuing bits of pumpkin flesh that are edible. Obviously overseeing the pumpkin carving as well, but I am a strong believer in showing children what to do, then letting them have a go, our pumpkin carving will never win any prizes, but even the six year old has a go, and has for a good number of years now.

Ingredients
1 white onion, chopped
As much pumpkin flesh as you can get from kid's pumpkins
1 butternut squash, chopped
1 carrot, chopped
1 pint/570ml of vegetable stock, using either a stock cube or stock pot
2-3tbsp olive oil
1 dash of cream (optional)

Method
Place the vegetables in a large pan with the olive oil on the wood-burner, when the vegetables are soft, add the stock, and simmer till ready. Add a dash of cream and serve with home-made bread rolls, see Chapter 5.

Toasted Marshmallows aka S'mores

My English version of an American tradition.

Not really a recipe, more of a tradition handed down from one generation to the next, I can remember making s'mores at Brownie and Guide camps as a child. The word s'more is simply a contraction of the phrase, 'some more' as these are particularly moreish treats. An American Scouting tradition dating back to the 1920s, a 's'more' or 'graham cracker sandwich', was made with two graham crackers, chocolate, and marshmallows roasted on an open campfire. I prefer to use chocolate digestives, as the biscuit and chocolate are already combined. Sadly being vegetarian I no longer eat marshmallows and have yet to find a good veggie alternative, but this hasn't stopped me introducing this classic to my children, who all but one love it.

Ingredients
1 bag of marshmallows
1 packet of chocolate digestive biscuits
Wooden skewers

Method
If you simply want to toast the marshmallows, place 2 or 3 on a wooden skewer and toast over the flames, till lightly browned on the outside, but not too long so the marshmallow starts dripping. To turn toasted marshmallows into s'mores, simply sandwich the marshmallows in between two chocolate digestives, making sure the chocolate is on the inside so the toasted marshmallow lightly melts the chocolate, and enjoy, sitting around the woodburner for an indoor, campfire treat.

CHAPTER 8
BASICS

All of the following recipes I have, and do make from time to
time, some like the home-made vanilla essence, I make a yearly
supply, eliminating the need to buy commercial essence; others
like pesto, pastry and houmous, I make occasionally when I
have either the time, or inclination.

Rough Puff Pastry
Pesto
Houmous
Vanilla Essence

Rough Puff Pastry

Puff pastry originated in France in 1645, where it was invented by an apprentice pastry cook by the name of Claudius Gele, in French it is known as pâte feuilletée or feuilletage. It is a light, layered, pastry that puffs up when cooked in the oven.

Making puff pastry is not difficult, but it is very time consuming, and personally I would recommend buying ready-made puff pastry whenever possible. I love cooking, but even I find this a rather laborious task as classic puff pastry can take 2-3 hours to prepare, and that doesn't include cooking time.

As a result, this recipe is for rough puff pastry, basically an easy way of making puff pastry, whereas in classic puff pastry you place a whole slab of butter on the dough, and fold and roll many times until you create 729 layers of folded dough, in this recipe, you pre-cut the butter, and roll 6-7 times, preparation time reduced to approximately 15 minutes.

Ingredients
2·7fl oz/79ml iced water
4 ½oz/125g plain flour
5oz/150g high quality butter, chopped into small cubes
¼ tsp of salt

Method
Combine the flour and salt, add the butter, using two knives, not your hands, cut the butter into the dough. Make a hole in the middle and pour in the water. Using a fork, mix together. Pour some flour onto a chopping board, and pat the dough onto it until it resembles a square shape. Roll out the dough into a rectangle about 10" / 25 ½cm long. Fold the bottom third into the middle, and the top third on top of the middle, rotate by ¼ and repeat. Do this at least 6 or 7 times. Wrap the dough in cling film and chill for at least 1 hour. After an hour, or overnight if you wish, the pastry is ready to use.

PESTO

Another Italian staple, my youngest has lived on pesto pasta since a baby, often requesting it for breakfast, lunch and dinner! However according to Consensus Action on Salt and Health (CASH), many of the commercial varieties contain 'more salt per serving than a McDonald's hamburger'. In some of the sauces, the pesto contained more than 1·5g of salt per 47·5g serving. This is another reason why making your own food, with the knowledge of what you are adding, is so important. Half the time we think we are eating healthily when in fact we are not.

Before you make this recipe, please note, 'pesto' comes from the Italian 'pestare' which simply means to crush or mash, so by all means use a food processor, if you have one, and electricity to use it, however, more traditionally, use a pestle and mortar. Even the word 'pestle' comes from the Italian 'pestare'.

Ingredients
½ clove crushed garlic
1 pinch of salt
3 handfuls of fresh basil
3 handfuls of pine nuts
1 handful of grated Parmesan
2-3 tbsp extra virgin olive oil
Squeeze of lemon juice

Method
First you will need to mix the nuts together with the basil, garlic, Parmesan, and olive oil and blend to a smooth paste in a food processor. However, if you are completely without power, do not own a food processor, or have the time or inclination to prepare food in a traditional manner, the order the ingredients are added becomes important.

In which case, combine the garlic and salt in the pestle and mortar until they become pastelike, then add the basil, small quantities at a time, grinding the leaves, next the pine nuts, once the pine nuts are suitably crushed add the Parmesan cheese, and finally the olive oil and lemon juice.

Houmous or Hummus

Let's start with the basics, houmous or hummus? 'Hummus' comes from the Arabic word meaning 'chickpeas' and the complete name of this dish is simply 'hummus bi tahina' which means 'chickpeas with tahini'. In America the spelling 'hummus' is popular, but in English 'houmous' is also quite commonplace. The reason for the confusion is that there is no consensus on how to translate Arabic words into English.

Much debate has been written on whether houmous is actually Middle Eastern or Greek? Both regions claim it to be their own, but the origins of a dish similar to 'hummus bi tahina' was written in Cairo in the 13th Century, however, no tahini or garlic appeared in the original recipe. As the Greeks and Egyptians were trade partners for centuries, they shared many foods, and thus both have been eating houmous for so long, in so many different variations, that the exact origin of the dish has been lost in antiquity.

Ingredients
1 tin cooked chickpeas
2 tbsp tahini
1 clove garlic, crushed
Squeeze of lemon juice
5 tbsp extra virgin olive oil
1 tsp cayenne pepper

Method

Firstly drain the chickpeas and add to the food processor, next add the garlic, tahini, lemon juice, and olive oil and blitz. Add more lemon juice, and possibly water, if needed.

But what if you don't have the use of a food processor, certainly back in the 13th Century, food processors weren't readily available! So it is quite possible to make houmous without such modern-day inventions.

As with pesto, houmous can be made using a pestle and mortar. Start by combining the garlic and salt in the pestle and mortar until they become pastelike, then add the chickpeas gradually, and continue to grind them into a paste, add the tahini and lemon juice, and a little water, if necessary, keep working the mixture until it reaches the required consistency. Place in a serving bowl, sprinkle the top with a little cayenne pepper and drizzle with olive oil.

Serve with vegetable crudités such as carrot, cucumber, celery, peppers etc. or warm flatbread.

Vanilla Essence

The vanilla pod is originally native to central Mexico and comes from the only fruit-bearing member of the orchid family. It was the ancient Indians from Mexico who first used the vanilla pods, but when defeated by the Aztecs, they lost control of the vanilla pod. Ironically the Aztecs were later defeated by the Spanish and they too lost control of the vanilla pod, the Spanish returned home with the vanilla beans which for a while were only used by the ruling classes, however, eventually they became popular throughout Europe.

Ingredients
8oz vodka
3-5 vanilla pods

Method
Slice the vanilla pods so the flavour can infuse into the vodka, add 3-5 vanilla pods per 8oz of vodka, pour the vodka into clean sterile bottles, either cleanse by pouring boiling water, or place through a dishwasher cycle, alternatively you can remove a little vodka from the bottle, and add the vanilla pods. Store in a cool, dark place for at least a month, and shake regularly. After one month the essence is ready, but the longer you leave it, the stronger the flavour. I then decant to smaller, prettier bottles and label them with the date made, but leave half a vanilla pod in each for extra infusion and aesthetics. However, you can strain the essence at this point if you prefer a clearer liquid. I no longer buy vanilla essence, making enough each Autumn not only to last the year, but also giving a few spare as Christmas gifts to friends, family and teachers. Vanilla essence is used as a flavouring particularly when baking cakes, see Chapter 6 for Chocolate Biscuit Cake Recipe.

CHAPTER 9
FORAGING

A lot has been written over the last few years on foraging, and I don't claim to be an expert on the subject. However, many of us forage without really even knowing it. Picking blackberries in the Autumn, elderflowers in the Spring. I have included a collection of my favourite foraging recipes. Although many of these recipes can be made on the woodburner, I would advise making these when you have power, to enjoy when you don't.

Stinging Nettle Soup
Elderflower Cordial
Elderflower Champagne
Elderberry Cordial
Sloe Vodka / Gin
Blackberry and Apple served with Greek Yogurt
Roasted Chestnuts
Spaghetti with Wild Garlic
Wild Venison Stew
Rosehip Syrup

STINGING NETTLE SOUP

Collecting the stinging nettles in early to mid Spring is the first adventure, it goes without saying that thick gloves should be worn. I have made this soup on many occasions, but the most memorable was for my son's 7th birthday, we celebrated by holding a bushcraft party in a small wooded section of a large London park. One of the games was 'I'm a Celebrity Bush Tucker trial' as well as the stinging nettle soup, we had chocolate crickets, elderflower cordial, chocolate raisins (we needed a few less obnoxious items for the fussy eaters!), we had a treasure hunt, the boys had to forage for their own sticks for the piñata. All in all it was a great success.

Ingredients
1lb/450g potatoes, chopped
½ lb/225g young stinging nettles, washed and roughly chopped
2oz/50g butter/margarine
1 pint/570ml of vegetable stock, using either a stock cube or stock pot
Sour cream to taste

Method
Cook the potatoes in a pan on the woodburner. Lightly fry the nettles in butter or margarine in a frying pan, making sure you only use the fresh young tops of the stinging nettles, you will need your gloves for this job. Boil some water to make stock, add the nettles and stock to the drained potatoes, and simmer gently. If you have the power, purée before serving, and add sour cream to taste. I like to serve with home-made bread rolls, see Chapter 5, and stinging nettle Gouda, another Dutch speciality, but Cheddar or normal Gouda will do just as well.

ELDERFLOWER CORDIAL

Elderflower is the blossom of the potentially poisonous Elder plant, which blooms from late May to mid July. The flowers are used as a flavouring in a variety of foods and drinks, but this is one of my favourites.

Home-made elderflower cordial, without any additives will keep in the fridge for a couple of weeks, however, if you add citric acid, it will last up to a year. Citric acid used to be readily available in pharmacies, unfortunately you cannot easily buy it over the counter anymore, you can however still purchase it from Amazon.

Ingredients
26 ½oz/750g sugar
2 ¾ pints/1·6l water
2 lemons, peeled and sliced (retaining both the peel and the slices)
20 elderflower heads
3 ½oz/85g citric acid (optional)

elderflower

Method

Remove the elderflowers from the stalks with a fork, and put to one side. Heat the sugar and water, until the sugar dissolves then remove from the heat, it is really important here that the liquid doesn't boil. Wash the flowers in cold water, shake and add to the sugar water, along with the lemon peel and sliced lemons and citric acid. Cover and leave for 24 hours.

Line a colander with a muslin, I still use the muslins my children used as babies, they have been thoroughly washed! But you can easily pick them up at any large supermarket or baby shop.

Pour the cordial through the muslin and colander, so you catch all the elderflower heads and lemon zest. Cleanse the bottles, either by pouring boiling water into them, putting them through a dishwasher cycle, or placing them in a low heat oven, obviously this is not possible without power. Using a funnel pour the cordial into the bottles, and enjoy.

ELDERFLOWER CHAMPAGNE

Champagne is actually a sparkling wine that is made from grapes grown only in the Champagne region of France, however, many people use the term 'Champagne' as a generic term for any sparkling wine, this is how I am using the term in this instance, therefore technically it is not 'Champagne' at all, but simply sparkling elderflower wine.

Ingredients

1 ¾oz/800g sugar
175fl oz/5l water
8 elderflower heads
4 lemons, zest and juice
½ tsp instant yeast

Method

Dissolve the sugar in approximately 70fl oz/2 litres of hot water in a fermenting bucket, if you have one, alternatively any large plastic bucket with a lid will do. Then top up with 105fl oz/3 litres of cold water. When cool add the elderflowers, having previously removed the elderflowers from the stalks with a fork, lemon zest and juice and yeast. Interestingly elderflowers do contain natural yeast and it is possible to make this champagne without the use of additional yeast, but to be on the safe side, I always add ½ tsp. Then leave to ferment for about a week.

After this time strain through a clean muslin, into a fresh fermentation bucket. Cover, then after a few hours decant into clean bottles with screw top or flip lids, such as Kilner jars. Cleanse the bottles, either by pouring boiling water into them, putting them through a dishwasher cycle, or placing them in a low heat oven and leave somewhere dark and cool for at least a fortnight.

ELDERBERRY CORDIAL

Elderberries are the fruit of the Elder tree, in fact the branches, leaves and twigs contain a small amount of cyanide, because of this, it is always recommended that you cook elderberries before consuming them. However, elderberries are renowned for their nutritional benefits which is why they have been part of traditional medicine for hundreds of years. It is from mid August to mid September that elderberries should be harvested, usually around the same time you are blackberrying.

Ingredients
Elderberries, as many as you can pick
Water, enough to cover the elderberries
1lb/450g sugar for every pint or 570ml of liquid
12 cloves for every pint or 570ml of liquid

elderberries

Method

Remove the elderberries from their stalks using a fork, simply cover with water and simmer for 20 minutes, this can be done on the wood-burner. Strain through a muslin. .

I haven't added quantities for the elderberries, pick as many as you can, cover with water, then measure the resulting liquid. For each pint of juice you make, add 1lb sugar and 12 cloves. Boil for a further 10 minutes, cool and bottle in clean bottles. I tend to pour boiling water in the bottles to cleanse them, but equally you can run them through the dishwasher or place them in a low heat oven. Once bottled I favour freezing the cordial, so I have home-made cordial all year round, but equally it can be drunk straight away. Obviously if you are without power, freezing is not an option.

Sloe Vodka/Gin

Sloes were one of the first fruits eaten by early man in Britain, evidence of this can be found in the excavation of a Neolithic village near Glastonbury in Somerset, where numerous sloe stones were unearthed, although I wouldn't recommend eating them myself as they are very acidic. Sloes are the fruit of the Blackthorn, a very prickly shrub or small tree, named accordingly due to its inch long black thorns.

Ingredients
1 pound sloes
4oz/110g sugar
1 litre vodka or gin

Sloes on blackthorn

Method
I favour freezing the sloes on the day they are picked, early Autumn is best, ideally after the first frost, which softens them, this eliminates the need to prick each sloe individually, which I have done in the past. Just remember to remove any stalks that may be on the berries. When you are ready to make the sloe vodka or gin, remove the sloes from the freezer, add them to the vodka or gin along with the sugar, making sure the vessel isn't too full and is watertight, otherwise you will waste a lot of this precious liquor. Simply shake daily for a period of two weeks, then bottle and leave to mature. A delicious festive gift or treat.

BLACKBERRY AND APPLE SERVED WITH GREEK YOGHURT

This is a real foraging recipe in our house as not only do we forage for the blackberries from late Summer to early Autumn, along the local hedgerows, we also happen to have an apple tree in the hedgerow opposite our house, so I can forage for those too. I don't forage for the Greek yoghurt!

Ingredients
9 oz/250 g blackberries
1 lb 2oz/500g cooking apples
2 ¼oz/55g sugar
Dollop of Greek yoghurt
Drizzle of honey (optional)

blackberries

Method
Peel, slice and core the apples, add to a pan with the blackberries and sugar, with just enough water to cover, simmer gently on the wood-burner. Serve with Greek yoghurt, a favourite in our house, add a drizzle of local honey, if you have been sparing with the sugar when cooking.

Roasted Chestnuts

Although this recipe is synonymous with Christmas and Bing Crosby, sweet chestnuts are available for foraging from late October through to the end of November. We are lucky enough to have our own small woodland with an abundance of sweet chestnut trees, but they are plentiful in the woodlands across Southern England. If you live further afield, they are readily available in supermarkets up and down the country. Like collecting conkers, a tradition with children that dates back to the 1850s, collecting sweet chestnuts is equally rewarding as you trample through the Autumnal woodland, looking for shiny brown nuts. But with sweet chestnuts, as opposed to their fraternal horse chestnuts, there is a culinary delight at the end.

Ingredients
Handful of sweet chestnuts

Method
Firstly soak the sweet chestnuts in lukewarm water for about half an hour to soften the skin and help loosen the fuzzy inner skin later on. If, when you make your incision the chestnut collapses in, then discard, they are probably rotten inside. Place them cut side up on a baking tray or roast in a chestnut roaster for about half an hour in the woodburner, you will need to keep the doors to the woodburner open and remember to keep the chestnuts moving regularly or they will burn. The chestnuts should open up when done.

SPAGHETTI WITH WILD GARLIC

This is a wonderful dish if you are a garlic lover. Wild garlic grows anytime between March and June in woodland areas and the aroma is phenomenal, often enticing me to pick enough leaves to make this dish, or throw in a salad.

Ingredients
1 bunch of wild garlic
1-2 cloves of garlic, crushed
10 ½oz/300g spaghetti
2-3 tbsp extra virgin olive oil
Handful of Parmesan

wild garlic

Method
Boil the spaghetti in a pan on the woodburner, once al dente, drain the spaghetti. Lightly fry the wild garlic and garlic together in the olive oil for just a couple of minutes, any longer and the leaves will become bitter, add the spaghetti to the garlic mix, sprinkle over freshly grated Parmesan and serve.

WILD VENISON STEW

We live in East Sussex, where there is an abundance of wild deer, so every now and then my husband brings home an entire deer, fortunately already butchered and ready to cook. As a vegetarian, I am not always as enthusiastic about this as my husband is, but I have experimented with venison steaks cooked on the griddle, a little dry apparently, to the following recipe which has become a firm family favourite. Venison is traditionally hunted from October to December, but can be frozen, if you have power, for a year round treat.

Is it a stew or casserole? In writing this book I decided once and for all to establish the difference between the two, and apparently the difference between a stew and a casserole is all in the cooking. A stew is traditionally cooked on the hob, a casserole is cooked in the oven.

Ingredients

2 venison steaks, chopped
1 onion, finely chopped
Handful of mushrooms
1 stick of celery, sliced
1 carrot, chopped
½ pinch of rosemary
½ pinch of thyme
½ pinch of garlic salt
2-3tbsp extra virgin olive oil
A sprinkling of plain flour

Method

Mix the flour, garlic salt and herbs together and toss the chopped steaks in the flour mixture. Then cook in the olive oil in a large pan on the woodburner until just brown, add some water and the vegetables and leave to simmer, stirring periodically. Serve with rice, potatoes or simply home-made bread to soak up the juices.

Rosehip Syrup

In the 1930s scientists discovered that the fruits or hips of the Dog Rose, contained more vitamin C than any other fruit or vegetable, in fact 1 cup of rosehip syrup contains more vitamin C than 40 oranges! During World War 2, when the UK was effectively cut off from the rest of the world, British children were given rosehip syrup which almost exclusively provided them with their daily requirements of the vitamin. The rosehips are best picked sometime between the end of August, and November, preferably after the first frost, which softens them.

Ingredients
Rosehips, as many as you can pick
Water, enough to cover the rosehips
11½oz/325g sugar for every 500ml rosehip syrup

rosehips

Method

Cleanse a couple of bottles by pouring boiling water over them then putting them in the oven on a low heat, if you are likely to make enough syrup to preserve.

Top and tail the rosehips, then roughly chop them and place in a large saucepan on the woodburner with boiling water, to cover them. Bring to the boil, then simmer for approximately 15 minutes.

Slowly strain the liquid through a muslin until all the juice is through, then repeat the process to ensure no pips are in the final cordial.

I haven't added quantities for the rosehips, pick as many as you can, cover with water, then measure the resulting liquid. For each pint of syrup you make, add the sugar accordingly. Heat slowly, stirring until the sugar has dissolved, then bring to the boil and boil for 3 minutes, removing any scum that may arise. Decant into the sterile bottles, when cool, label the bottles, and use within four months. Once opened the cordial should be refrigerated.

Rosehip syrup is delicious as an accompaniment to porridge or Greek yoghurt (a family favourite), it can also be poured over pancakes or vanilla ice cream.